HEAL-THY MIND-BODY

Your Guide to Healing with Intention, Insight, and Guided Imagery

Gentle Guidance for Mental Clarity and Emotional Release through Hypnosis

Liza Boubari

Copyright © 2025 Liza Boubari

All rights reserved. No part of this book may be reproduced or transmitted in any form or by any means, electronic or mechanical, including photocopying, recording, or by any information storage and retrieval system, without the express written permission of the publisher or author, except for the inclusion of brief quotation in a review.

The material in this book is intended for informational purposes only and is not a substitute for medical attention. By reading this, you, the reader, assume all risk for any advice given here and how you use it.

For authorized copies of this document, please contact HealWithin.com or (818) 551-1501. Enjoy reading.

ISBN 978-1-7333126-7-7 (print)

ISBN 978-1-7333126-8-4 (epub)

Library of Congress Control Number: 2025901653

Second Edition

Published by HealWithin, Inc.
330 Arden Ave Suite 130
Glendale CA 91203
www.healwithin.com

Dedication

This book is dedicated to all those, especially women, seeking to heal from within—to discover intention, insight, and clarity on their journey to wholeness.

You Matter

To my beloved grandmother and mother, who instilled in me the values of grace, compassion, and healthful living. Your lessons on elegance, proper conduct, and self-care have shaped my mission to help others heal and thrive.

You Matter.
With love and honor,

Liza

NOTHING HAPPENS BY CHANCE

Do you agree?

The fact that you are holding this book is no coincidence. You are here because you are ready—ready to reconnect with your deeper self, align with the universal energy that flows through all things, and embark on a journey of healing and transformation.
I believe spiritual awakening begins the moment you realize you are part of something greater than yourself. Some call it God, the universe, Source, or Consciousness—it doesn't matter what name you give it. What matters is recognizing that this energy is guiding you and that you are not alone.
Through this book, you will uncover tools and insights to harmonize your mind, body, and spirit, empowering you to heal from within and embrace the life you truly desire.

"Healing begins when we allow ourselves to feel, to release, and to trust the process." ~ Liza

Table of Contents

INTRODUCTION 1
MY STORY 3
YOUR STORY 6
THE BOUBARI 3E METHOD 7
EVOKE 8
YOU WANT CHANGE - BE THE CHANGE 9
INSIDE YOUR MIND 13
YOUR MIND IN ACTION 15
LISTEN TO YOUR BODY TALK 25
THE MASKS YOU WEAR 27
EMBRACE 30
EMOTIONAL EATING 31
TAKE THIS TO BED! 35
FEARS AND PHOBIAS – REAL OR IMAGINED? 38
UNLEARNING FEARS 41
SELF ACTUALIZATION 43
BEING HAPPY IS A STATE OF MIND 50
EVOLVE 52
GUIDED RELAXATION 53
RELAXATION TECHNIQUES 65
LAUGHTER IS GOOD MEDICINE 67
TALK THE TALK 69
TIPS TO LIVING HEALTHIER AND HAPPIER 71
FOODS TO KEEP YOU HEALTHY, FRUITY, NUTTY 73
LIZA'S '33 DAY' HABIT FORMING THEORY: 77
BONUS: A GENTLE SELF-HYPNOSIS PRACTICE FOR DEEPER HEALING 85
ABOUT LIZA 87

*"Transform your fears, anxiety, and pain to stand UP and go beyond your desired dreams and expectations. You can either focus on what is tearing you apart – or what is holding you together.
Choose You – You Matter"* ~ Liza

INTRODUCTION

This booklet is an accumulation of my thoughts. These short reads are about Heal-thy Mind-Body healing, guided imagery, and hypnosis – as if a window to your inner workings of our mind-body-spirit to realize, expand, see, and create change within. In a nutshell, to Evoke passion, Embrace femininity, and Evolve spiritually.

Also, most of what you read is my interpretation of what I believe in and use in my daily life and practice. The purpose of this booklet is to remind you of the tools you already have and possess within you, and that you have been equipped with from birth to now. I urge you to continue your pursuit of discovery and practice in internal-external wellness!

We must live in the joy of a promise and recall that for every human being, their perception and programming is what their world consists of –until they decide to amend it.

I will mention a lot about 'Living Victoriously-You Matter'. The essence of all living is to live with a purpose, a sense of accomplishment, and self-respect, realizing that how you value your life is mainly yours alone and that no one can do, say, or feel for you. That no one truly has power over you or controls you. Even the slightest shift in the way you perceive events can cause incredible changes in how you act and react, which is stunning and miraculous. Events that have in the past caused you discomfort, grief, hurt, anguish, or rage can suddenly remind you of your strength and focus now. Some of these insights can be a trigger, but more importantly, bring wonderment and joy within.

The only rule to this is: There are no rules to change….
but a Choice. Healing is a Choice. Standing Up for yourself is a choice - Your Choice. Consider this booklet a bridge between your conscious acting mind and your subconscious feeling mind – or simply put, "a guide". Use the suggestions and exercises that work best for you, and the rest will fall into place, naturally.

Living Victoriously - "You Matter"

Liza

MY STORY

Greetings, I'm Liza, the founder of HealWithin.com.

My story is one many women can relate to. As humans—especially women—we carry layers of stories, each one contributing to who we are. Some stories we share with others, while others keep silent. But each of these stories holds power.

In 1985, I underwent surgery to remove an 8.7-centimeter ovarian cyst. Two years later, another cyst developed, leading to yet another surgery. By the time I was divorced, working two jobs, and carrying the heavy weight of unaddressed stress, I developed yet another cyst.

I remember that day so clearly in my doctor's office, where, due to the rapid growth of my previous cysts, the recommendation was to schedule surgery within the month. As the tears welled up, my throat tightened, and I remembered my last surgery. I had placed my hand over my stomach and silently told my body, *The next time we go into the operating room, it will be to bring life into the world.*

With that memory in mind and my thoughts of a different future, I decided: I could not put my body through another surgery.

With the encouragement of an acupuncturist, I turned to hypnotherapy. After just four sessions, the cyst was gone. During those sessions, I discovered why my body created those cysts—and I believe I healed myself.

This profound healing experience sparked my passion to explore the science of hypnosis. In 1997, after completing my studies with renowned clinical hypnotherapist Gil Boyne, I left my career in law to dedicate myself to hypnotherapy. Since then, my mission has been to help others heal from within.

Throughout my career as a clinical hypnotherapist, I've learned that our bodies are truly magical, and our minds are sharp and resilient. Each part of us is connected to our emotions, and those emotions have the power to create and to heal. Our bodies and minds work miracles every day, even if we aren't always aware of them. Over the years, I have specialized in women's issues, and one thing I've learned is that we are all beautiful, powerful creatures. We are all connected, intertwined, and one.

At HealWithin, we help you heal from within. From the moment you step in, you've already made the unconscious decision to begin your transformation. The change you seek is in your hands—and it starts here, today.

I've created this guide to help you stay healthy in mind and body. I'm deeply passionate about sharing my knowledge, so others can thrive too. Whether you're navigating doubts, pain, or challenges, I am here with you every step of the way. Now, you stand at the threshold of your journey. Just like everything in life, you have two choices: skim the surface, or dive in deep and commit fully to transforming your health, mind, body, and spirit. This is a lifestyle transformation—and it's within your reach.

These lessons are not just something to read; they're tools to exercise, practice, and embody. Your commitment will benefit your body and soul. **It's going to be easy. Effortless. Even fun.**

To celebrate the new you, you must be fearless and bold. You must learn to tap within, declare your intentions, and stop negative self-talk. Recognize and validate your emotions and fears, then stand up. Stand up to *evoke* your passion, *embrace* your femininity, and *evolve* spiritually.

This year, I also started *Real-Talk with Liza*—a platform designed to make a bigger impact, one conversation, one guest at a time. Through every episode, we dive into meaningful discussions with inspiring people who share powerful insights, all with the aim of helping you live your life fully and authentically.

YOUR STORY

A new cycle begins this day, yet a new cycle begins every day. Indeed, every moment. So, if you recognize anything on this day, recognize what it symbolizes: The miracle of the endlessly continuing Cycle of Life. What a grand day! What a time for celebration!

We begin again today! We turn the page!

And so, let go of all that you do not wish to carry with you any further. Any fear, any sadness, any anger, any resentment, any disappointment, any lament...let it all go. Every story, every chapter was written with this day in mind. You wrote it a long time ago when the spirit within you decided to live this life, exactly as it is -- with all the pains and sufferings, with all the laughter and joys, with every breath and every ounce of your being.

You are here - you arrived at this page - here and now. Now, evoke your passion. Evoke what was only to remember but not to live by; Embrace your femininity and your feminine self, embracing the present; and Evolve spiritually - transform to what you desire to be as a springboard to living victoriously. Get on with Life!

> *"The tragedy of life doesn't lie in not reaching your goal. The tragedy lies in having no goals to reach."* ~ Liza

THE BOUBARI 3E METHOD

The Boubari 3E Method is more than just a framework—it's a transformative journey that empowers you to reconnect with your essence and rewrite your story.

The 3E Message
When you look in the mirror, see beyond the reflection. Greet your inner child, honor your journey, and release unrealistic expectations. Validate your inherent beauty, recognize your God-given gifts, and embrace the truth of who you are. Your story is uniquely yours, and you have the power to shape it.

3 is a number rich in meaning: it represents the Trinity and the unity of Mind, Body, and Emotions. It reminds us that while we are interconnected, we are also beautifully unique. E stands for both my given name, Elizabeth, and the transformative steps of The Boubari 3E method:

- Evoke the past—acknowledge the history that has shaped your experiences.
- Embrace the present—accept the reality of who you are now with grace and compassion.
- Evolve into your future—step boldly into the life you desire and deserve.

Evoke what was - Embrace what is - Evolve to what will be…You Matter

Evoke

YOU WANT CHANGE - BE THE CHANGE

Let's have a moment of reflection.
Have you ever felt a constant pull toward negative thoughts?
Have they overshadowed the gratitude you want to feel,
leaving you caught in a cycle of self-doubt and unworthiness?

When negativity becomes a go-to response, it not only weighs on your heart—it can weigh you down, harming your health and leading to issues like depression.

The good news? Negativity is learned. Which means – it can be unlearned. You *can* change your thoughts. And when you do, you can change your life. Trust me—I've walked this path.

Happiness doesn't just happen to us; it's something we choose, over and over, each day.
We all feel stuck sometimes, caught in what we think is broken and personal. But staying in that place is a choice—and so is moving forward.

Healing is a journey that asks you to shift your perspective, to release what no longer serves you. Choose happiness.
Not only does it come with a lighter heart, but it opens the door to laughter, joy, and a deeper connection with life.

Remember, falling in love when you're lonely is like grocery shopping when you're hungry. You end up with a lot in your cart that you do not need. And when you are on a healthy streak and in wellness, you only shop the outside parameters and healthy choices.

What if, through the tools and techniques in this book, you learn to love who you are, embrace your worth, and trust that you are enough? When you feel complete on your own, you'll find the person who truly deserves all that you are. So go after the things that make your heart race, lift your spirit, and make you the best version of yourself. Be the change you're longing for, and watch as your world transforms in ways you never imagined.

How You Treat Yourself—and People—That Matters Most

How you show up for yourself and others shapes your life. We all need love, kindness, human touch, and laughter to truly thrive. When you share these gifts, you nurture not only the souls around you but your own as well.

I've come to realize that what we see is only part of the story. What if you become a witness to your life? It's as if you are watching a movie. What if you stop judging or comparing? Appearances can often be deceptive. Others show only what they want you to see, so avoid comparing yourself to anyone else. Remember, those who feel confident and comfortable in their skin do not live life by comparison but by analyzing, only to become better. Instead, look within—ignite your desires, build from your passions, and live in a way that brings you joy.

Remember, the grass isn't greener elsewhere—it's greenest where *you* water it. Tend to your soul, feed your spirit, and follow your light.

Life doesn't always introduce you to the people you wish for; sometimes, it gives you exactly who you need. These are the people who will teach you, challenge you, love you, and even hurt you—but they will all shape you, preparing you to become who you're meant to be. Life is 90% mental, 10% physical. If you can see it in your mind, you can make it real. Your only limits are the ones you set for yourself.

And finally, keep looking forward. If Cinderella had gone back to pick up her shoes, her story would have been very different. Today, you can let go of what's behind you and step into life waiting just ahead.

Your mantra: **I now "*Evoke my passion, Embrace my femininity and Evolve spiritually –"I Matter"***

Strengthen your heart with love and compassion.

Walking on eggshells is one of the worst feelings you can have and one of the worst feelings you can create for someone else.

Nobody likes walking on eggshells. Life's too short for eggshells. When the fear of things staying the same exceeds the fear of failure...anything can happen. Be open to change. Invite the unknown and create the life you desire. You can't be fearful and grateful simultaneously.

Loving yourself means embracing a relationship where love and safety are woven into every moment—where you can feel free to be *yourself* without fear or doubt. If you find yourself walking on eggshells, holding back words or parts of who you are, remember that true love doesn't demand that you shrink or silence yourself. Instead, love allows you to flourish, to feel seen and heard, valued and safe.

You deserve a love that doesn't leave you questioning your worth, a love that lifts you. Start with compassion for yourself, knowing you are enough just as you are. In choosing to honor yourself, you open the door to a love that truly cherishes you. This is YOUR story...YOUR journey. Live Victoriously - make it AMAZING!

INSIDE YOUR MIND

The concept of three levels of mind is nothing new. Sigmund Freud, the famous Austrian psychologist, was probably the first to popularize it into mainstream society as we know it today. Freud created a useful model of the mind, which he separated into three tiers or sections—the conscious mind or ego, the

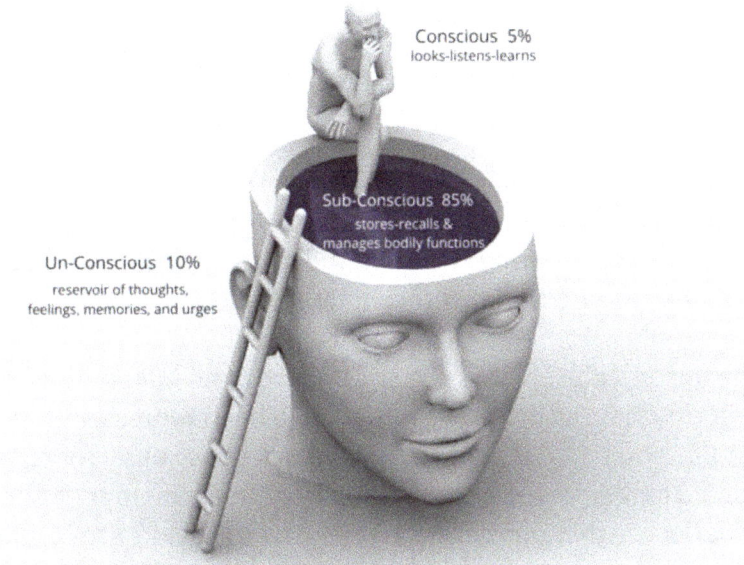

preconscious, and the unconscious mind.

The best way to illustrate the concept of the three minds is by using to illustrate.
Your conscious mind occupies the top, representing about 5% of your brain capabilities.
Mid-level (inside) is a slightly larger section that is referred to as the subconscious. It accounts for about 80% of your brain's capabilities.

The unconscious mind. It occupies the base and fills out the other 10% of your brain capabilities.

How They Work Together

Your conscious mind is what most people associate with who you are because that is where most people live day to day. Consciously, you "look-listen-learn". Your conscious mind is the part that gives out orders. It communicates to the outside world and the inner self through speech (verbal), pictures (visual), writing, physical movement (Kinesthetic or touch), and thought.

The subconscious mind "stores information, recalls information, and regulates your entire bodily functions." It is in charge of your recent memories and is in continuous contact with the resources of the unconscious mind.

The unconscious mind is the storehouse of all memories and past experiences, both those that have been repressed through trauma and those that have simply been consciously forgotten and no longer important to us. It's from these memories and experiences that our beliefs, habits, and behaviors are formed. The unconscious provides us with the meaning of all our interactions with the world, as filtered through our beliefs and habits. It communicates through feelings, emotions, imagination, sensations, and dreams.

*"It's not the load that breaks you down.
It's the way you carry it."* ~ **Lou Holtz**

YOUR MIND IN ACTION

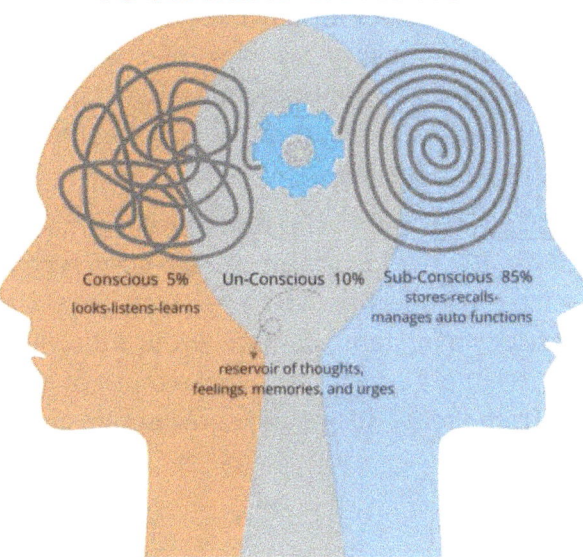

The following analogy may help to clarify the concept of how the three minds work a little more. If you imagine your mind is like a computer ...

Your <u>conscious</u> mind is best represented by the keyboard and monitor. Data is inputted on the keyboard, and the results are thrown up on the monitor screen. That is how your conscious mind works – information is taken in via some outside (or internal) stimulus from your environment, and the results are thrown up instantaneously into your consciousness.

Your <u>subconscious</u> is like the RAM in your computer. For those who don't know, RAM is the place in a computer where programs and data that are currently in use are kept so they can be reached quickly by the computer processor. It is much faster than other types of memory, such as the hard disk or CD-

ROM. Your subconscious works in the same way. Any recent memories are stored there for quick recall when needed, such as your telephone number or the name of a person you just met. It also holds your current programs that you run every day, such as your current recurring thoughts, behavior patterns, habits, and feelings.

Your <u>unconscious</u> is like the hard disk drive (the main chip) in your computer. It is the long-term storage place for all your memories and programs that have been installed since birth. Your unconscious mind (and ultimately your subconscious mind) then uses these programs to make sense of all the data you receive from the world and to keep you safe and ensure your survival.

The Conscious Mind

The conscious mind is where you do all your thinking and logical reasoning.

Take, for example, when you were a baby. Your conscious mind has not yet developed enough to test and measure all the information from your environment, so at this age, it sits in the background and it's your subconscious and unconscious that do all the data gathering and reasoning – identifying that the bottle or nipple is a source of food, that crying gets you attention, that cuddles from mum mean you are safe.

In this stage, it's your other two minds hard at work forming logical patterns of association (habits, beliefs, and emotions) that help you to survive. By far the best explanation is … Its ability to direct your focus and the ability to imagine that is not real.

Directing Your Focus

While your subconscious mind has a much stronger sense of awareness of your surroundings than your conscious mind (some suggest it's where your "sixth sense" comes from) and is always switched on, even when asleep, it just obeys orders from your conscious mind. This ability of your conscious mind to direct your attention and awareness is one of the most important powers you have. It can be used for good or evil, for constructive or destructive means. We alone can choose how we are going to respond to our experiences in life.

Using Your Imagination

The other important ability of the conscious mind is the use of visualization. Your mind can imagine something that is new and unique – something you've never physically experienced before. By contrast, your subconscious can only offer versions of what memories it has stored of your past experiences. The best part is - the subconscious mind can't distinguish between that which the conscious mind imagines and that which is real, so whatever is brought up by conscious imagination and intently focused upon also brings forth the emotions and feelings that are associated with that image in your mind for you to experience.

"If you can imagine it, you can create it" or *"What you perceive- your mind can conceive."*

The Role of the Subconscious

Apart from short-term memory, the subconscious also plays an important role in our day-to-day functioning. It works hard at ensuring you have everything you need for quick recall and access to when you need it - the filter. Things like –
- Memories – such as what your telephone number is, how to drive a car without having to consciously think about it, what you need to get from the shop on the way home, etc.
- Current programs you run daily, such as behaviors, habits, and mood.
- Filters (such as beliefs and values) to run information through to test their validity according to your perception of the world.
- Sensations are taken in via your 5 senses, and what they mean to you

One of the truly great things about the subconscious (and one which we need to take advantage of to affect change) is ... it obeys orders! such as "sleep now."

The Role of the Unconscious

In many respects, the unconscious deals with all the same tasks as the subconscious – memory, habits, feelings, emotions, and behaviors. The difference between the two minds, however, is that the unconscious is the source of all these programs that your subconscious uses. It is the place where all your memories and experiences since birth have been stored. It's from these memories that your beliefs, habits, and behaviors are formed and reinforced over time.

8 RULES OF THE SUBCONSCIOUS MIND

RULE 1 – Thoughts combined with emotion create a physical change –
Thoughts affect the functions of the body and thus cause a physical reaction. For instance, if you worry this can cause ulcers, if you have anger, this activates adrenal glands, if you have anxiety and fear, this increases your pulse rate. Any idea or thought that has emotional content will cause a physical reaction.

The subconscious mind is the feeling mind. This physical reaction can become an adversary in your life, so to eliminate this adversary, we must work with the subconscious mind and change the idea that is responsible for this physical reaction.

Liza guides you on how to eliminate the negative or adversarial thoughts that cause negative physical reactions

RULE 2 – What is Expected Tends to Be Realized –
A very powerful rule for those who are success-oriented. The Brain and the Nervous System only respond to MENTAL IMAGES. It doesn't matter if the mental image is self-induced or from an external view.

The mental image is embedded in the neuropathways, and the subconscious mind uses every means at its disposal to carry out the plan. That MENTAL IMAGE is the plan. Usually, the image is created by your words, and then by REPETITION is the subconscious.

RULE 3 – Imagination is more Powerful –
Knowledge or Reason when dealing with your mind or the mind of another – Wow, what a rule huh? Imagination is more powerful than knowledge…when dealing with your mind or the mind of another…the mind of another part is critical to all you sales professionals, as it deals with the power of persuasion. Reason is always overruled by imagination. Imagination is more powerful than knowledge or reason.

Liza teaches you how to utilize the emotion that attaches to your imagination to get you where you want to go. He shows you how to store mental images in the subconscious (the feeling mind). Your IMAGINATION is either an ally or an adversary.

Those who master the power of persuasion or who influence others are highly paid. The 'ole saying that 'teachers are paid a little, but influences are paid a lot' still holds today.

RULE 4 – Opposing Ideas Cannot be Held at the same time –
Your subconscious mind is incapable of holding opposing ideas at the same time. Now that does not mean you can't have more than one idea in your memory, and go back and forth, but those ideas cannot be held simultaneously.

If you do not understand this rule, this can cause severe frustration or anger. For example, if you teach your children to be honest in their daily lives, but you are not honest in your business, this is an incongruency that creates justification for you. You seek to justify dishonesty by saying something like, 'Well, my competitors do it, I need to support my family'.

This creates conflict and stress. Why are you feeling stressed? Because of your subconscious conflict of being incongruent every single day. Your self-talk will support your justification. Liza teaches you how to reprogram to eliminate this incongruency.

RULE 5 – Once an idea is accepted by the subconscious mind, it remains until replaced by another idea –
The longer an idea remains, the more difficult it becomes to replace it with a new idea. This ties in to reprogramming your subconscious in one of the 3 ways: REPETITION, AUTHORITY FIGURE, or TRAUMATIC EXPERIENCE.

For example, if you are overweight and have been so for quite some time, it'll be difficult to permanently lose that weight without some reprogramming. You're likely overweight through repetition, so your new idea to get in shape is opposed to your repetition of being overweight. Liza's Stand Up to Slim Down program can help you move beyond this.

RULE 6 – An Emotionally Induced Symptom Will Cause Organic Physical Change if it persists long enough –
If you fear ill health (i.e., I have a nervous stomach, I have a tension headache), you will eventually develop ill health. It's not your ill health affecting you, it's an infected mind causing ill health.

RULE 7 – Each Suggestion that is acted upon creates less opposition to the successive suggestion –
This is also a very powerful rule, one of the top 3...
this is a trend, a mental trend...if you have acted upon a suggestion, then the next suggestion will be easier for you...for example, if you want to go from a $5,000 per month income to $8,000 per month...your subconscious mind has already accepted the $5,000 per month, now it's easier to accept the programming to increase that income... change your mindset from the core.

RULE 8 – The greater the conscious effort, the less the subconscious responds –
If you attempt to grab water with sheer force, you will have no water in your clenched fist. But, if you cup your hand to hold the water you will have a hand full of water...the clenched fist (the conscious effort) vs. the cupped hand (the programmed subconscious)... the programming works fine without you, so get out of your way... stop forcing it to happen, just let it happen...(you can't force yourself to calm down, just let it happen).

You do not necessarily have to memorize the rules, just be aware of them, and where they affect your life, whether positively or negatively.

If you want to affect change in your life at a core level, then you will have to work on the programs that are held in the subconscious and unconscious mind. There are specialized ways to make that happen. By continuously being in charge of your thoughts through directing your focus and using visualization, you can influence what programs the subconscious mind constantly runs. Do the same thing over and over for 33 consecutive days (and with enough emotional energy) then it will start to reprogram your unconscious internal representation and belief system. And when that happens, you'll experience change on a very deep level!

The use of hypnotherapy is another way to tap within...a journey to your inner mind

Liza teaches you how to master your subconscious mind to help you improve yourself, your relationships, and your life. Because… You Matter!

"You cannot change the world overnight. But you can change how you show up in it from the core; calm, clear, and centered. When you heal within, you shift how you respond to what you put into the world."
~ Liza

LISTEN TO YOUR BODY TALK

Your body does and can communicate with you, such as when you feel hot, cold, pleasure, or pain. Yet when you go to work, out with your friends and family, sleep, eat, dance, and live your life, you are likely to take your body for granted. Oftentimes, people don't pay attention to their bodies.

You may even stuff your emotions into your body. Once in a while, you may pretend the pain and the hurt you feel are not there. You can ignore them for a while, but eventually, they will surface in ways that may be familiar but undesirable.

Maybe most of your life, your feelings, wants, and desires became confused or controlled by other people's needs and expectations. What about now? Are you ready to start taking control of your life? Are you ready to take the time to become more caring and more responsible for who you are? To begin living your life for yourself, respecting and appreciating who *you* are?

You can begin by letting go of old habits that have been blocking your true feelings. Let go of unhealthy habits that have supported and cushioned you to this day. Let go of habits that have become a buddy system to you and have since been working to your detriment. For example, smoking, overeating, oversleeping, drugs, alcohol, gambling, insomnia, and anorexia... suppressing and causing you to deny your true self.

Begin by creating or finding a safe place. This may be your own room, your backyard, or a friend's house. Remember, as you let go of your old habits that mask your feelings, you may begin to experience or feel the tension behind or beneath those habits. You may even tend to avoid the underlying feelings and resume your old habits- yet it's ok to allow the suppressed, hurt, or angry feelings to surface. Become sensitive to what is happening within your physical and emotional body. Let your feelings out, scream, cry, or laugh. Let the knots of tension go. Knowing that it's going to be hard at first, *it's time to listen to your body talk*. It's time to trust and accept your true self.

THE MASKS YOU WEAR

A mask is an identity you wear at different moments throughout the day. It is a habitual way of expressing yourself in your daily life. Like most of us, you may be aware that you act and react towards people differently depending on the situation. Although it is not a different you, it is what you portray yourself to be.

Ever notice how we have a different "mask" for every situation? There's the "Oh, I understand" mask we wear in meetings, the "I love being here" mask we throw on at family gatherings, and the "I'm completely calm and relaxed" mask we wear when everything's falling apart.

How many masks do you wear?

Ordinarily, a person wears approximately five to ten masks a day, if not more. These masks are of different types. There are at least two or more types of personality masks: everyday masks and concealing masks.

Imagine this: You're interacting with a whole cast of characters in just 15 minutes—your partner in one room, your child in another, the neighbor outside, and then finally the cashier at the store. Each encounter requires a slightly different "you." You may even catch yourself slipping into different roles, wearing different "masks" as you adapt to each situation.

These masks we wear can feel like armor—like layers of protection we don't even realize we're putting on. They're part of our lives: the careful smile, the accommodating nod, the brave front, and sometimes, the urge to make ourselves smaller or louder than we truly feel inside. And sure, these "masks" can help us get through the day. But after a while, they start to feel heavy, and sometimes, you might find yourself thinking, "Who am I beneath all these layers?"

Do you ever wonder why you feel stuck, or why you can't seem to find what truly makes you happy? Have you ever asked yourself, "Why do I feel like I'm living someone else's life?" These questions are part of the journey of discovering the masks we wear and understanding why they're there. Often, these masks aren't just habits—they're survival tactics we learned over time, ways we adapted to handle difficult relationships, past hurts, expectations, and fears.

Here's the truth: These masks don't define you. They aren't your true self. Beneath them, you have a beautiful, authentic essence—one that deserves to be seen and celebrated. And yes, removing these masks can feel vulnerable, even scary. But it's also profoundly freeing.

The subconscious mind plays a powerful role here, holding onto patterns long after they've served their purpose. Hypnosis offers a way to gently slip past that internal guard, reaching into the subconscious to release old, unhelpful patterns. Through hypnosis, you can invite new, empowering beliefs and release the masks that no longer serve you. The result? A more harmonious, complete version of you—one that feels true, joyful, and free.

Imagine weight lifting and having the freedom to simply *be* without pretense. Yes, it can be hard, but the relief and wholeness you'll feel are more than worth it. Letting go of these layers is not just possible; it's a gift you can give yourself—one that lets you fully step into your life as the person you were always meant to be.

You *can* take it off - you can be bold - you can be vulnerable - You can be FREE to be You. At any moment, you could choose to make a new choice and be the better person you desire. Which moment will you choose? The choice is yours.

Embrace

EMOTIONAL EATING

What gets in the way of your ability to lose weight? Lack of willpower to stick to a healthy eating and exercise routine? The intense influence of advertisements urging you to eat unhealthy foods? Lack of interest? Not knowing how to lose weight.

The answer, according to a new survey of psychologists, suggests that when it comes to dieting, weight loss, and weight gain, <u>emotions</u> play a central role and may be the primary obstacle to weight loss. Have you ever felt guilty after eating a cookie and then decided to eat the whole box, since you'd already blown your diet? Have you felt low and skipped exercise? Then you've experienced emotions interfering with your weight loss.

Understanding and managing the behaviors and emotions related to weight management is essential to weight loss. If you are overweight, it is because your brain has a reason for it. If you try to force yourself to lose weight, you are waging war against your brain. This is a war you are bound to lose!

Again, it all relates to stress. The primitive brain doesn't understand modern stress. It interprets stress according to ancient programs. Modern stress is interpreted by the primitive brain as immediate physical danger, famine, or susceptibility to the elements, such as frigid temperatures. It responds with measures appropriate to the perceived danger. If your chronic stress is consistently interpreted as physical danger, your brain will want you to be lean and agile, so you are more prepared to fight or flee. This is why some people cannot gain weight no matter how much they eat. Their brains have a reason to keep them thin.

If your brain interprets stress as potential famine, however, it will demand that you eat while you can. It will also slow your metabolism, enabling you to gain weight as quickly as possible. It needs you to be fat, and if you try to be thin, you are setting yourself up for failure.

The key is to identify the underlying, chronic stressors in your life. For some, emotional trauma is the cause. For others, physical causes such as sleep apnea or insomnia are at the root of the problem. For others, a stressful or mismatched relationship may be at the root of the issue. Whatever the cause of the stress that your brain interprets as famine is the key to reprogramming your mind and body to agree to be thin.

The source of hope for weight loss success and a more conscious, mindful existence is to identify and learn to let go of underlying issues so that you are not continually fighting an uphill emotional battle.

Our Stand Up to Slim Down program is designed to help you be at your best!

Emotions Trigger Cravings
Emotional eating often stems from using food to cope with feelings like stress, sadness, boredom, or even happiness. These emotions trigger cravings for comfort foods, often high in sugar, fat, or salt.

It's Not About Hunger
Unlike physical hunger, which builds gradually and can be satisfied with any food, emotional hunger feels urgent and specific. It's tied to emotional needs rather than physical ones.

Temporary Comfort, Lasting Guilt
While eating may provide temporary relief or distraction, it often leads to feelings of guilt, shame, or frustration afterward, creating a cycle of emotional eating and negative emotions.

Awareness Is Key
Identifying triggers is the first step to breaking the cycle of emotional eating. Keeping a journal or practicing mindfulness can help recognize patterns and distinguish emotional hunger from physical hunger.

Healthy Alternatives Work
Replacing food with healthier coping mechanisms can help address the underlying emotion without resorting to eating. Building emotional resilience and finding non-food-related sources of comfort are essential steps to overcoming emotional eating.

> *To be fully in touch with who you are – listen you're your entire being and embrace the whole you. "You Matter"*

TAKE THIS TO BED!

Since the turn of the Century, it has been recognized that stress can precipitate chronic disease, and any doctor could tell you that stress sets off complex and destructive reactions in the nervous and hormonal systems. Insomnia has been recognized as one of the symptoms of stress.

More than 42% of our population suffers from insomnia. Each year, more than a billion sleeping pills are sold. This should give you some idea of how many people are unable to sleep without having to resort to drugs.

Here are some facts for you.

1. Taking worrisome troubles to bed with you.
You cannot expect to get a good night's sleep if you lie awake worrying about problems. The roof is leaking, work is piling up on your desk, the curtains are not being hung, your daughter's prom dress needs alteration, next week's interview, etc. Whether you're a lawyer, physician, politician, stay-at-home mom, or business executive, you must learn to lock your troubles in a box before you go to bed. At least you should keep them out of the bedroom.

Why not think about them while watching TV and shut them off when you turn off the TV?

2. Obsessed with the false idea that you just can't sleep.
Stop counting sheep - the more you count, the more you are using your logical mind.

3. Tension fatigue
Going to bed feeling over-fatigued may cause you to be sleepless. Excess fatigue toxins tend to stimulate the brain.

4. Sexual incompatibility in marriage
It would be a serious omission not to include under the causes of insomnia the many husbands and wives who are unable to sleep well because of sexual problems. Wives who are deprived of sex satisfaction, love, and affection are often restless. Husbands who are rejected by their wives often complain of an inability to sleep. Couples who bicker and quarrel just before going to bed aren't going to enjoy a good night's rest.

5. Guilty feelings.
Going to bed with a bad conscious. Worrying during the night about what he or she did or said is a trigger. Some women cry because of hurt and feelings, which naturally keep them awake. Guilt causes fear. Fear can bring on anxiety, and in turn, anxiety can result in insomnia.

6. Pain and discomfort from some illness.
You can't expect to sleep well if you are experiencing some physical pain, such as an abscessed tooth or a severe headache. Remedy the pain and you'll fall into a deep sleep.

7. Bad sleeping conditions.
A hard mattress and a bad pillow can be a major cause of an infant crying at night. Telephone calls, someone snoring in the room.

Here are some tips and solutions:

- Leave the worries out of your bed.
- I am safe.
- If you wake up, remain in bed. Keep your eyes closed and stop worrying about not being able to sleep. Sleep will come.
- There is nothing I can do about it now - I will tend to them when I awaken.
- Command your mind to "sleep now." (just like when you were told as a kid)
- Positive suggestions: "I am to sleep soundly and awaken in the morning feeling refreshed and invigorated".

FEARS AND PHOBIAS – REAL OR IMAGINED?

We've all experienced it—that churning stomach, racing heart, or sweaty palms that grip us when faced with something that triggers fear. For some, it's standing in front of a crowd to speak; for others, it's creepy crawly insects, the fear of death, or even emotional vulnerability. Fear, whether real or imagined, always stems from emotions or experiences deeply rooted in our lives.

Take Janet, for instance. She dreads going to the dentist. The mere thought of a needle or her nervousness builds up until she's nearly hyperventilating by the time she arrives. This reaction isn't logical—it's fueled by a phobia, an irrational fear that creates avoidance and anxiety even in non-threatening situations.

How Fear Takes Root

Phobias often originate from a single frightening event, whether personally experienced or witnessed. For example, a parent's fear of water or dogs might inadvertently teach their child to avoid those things. Watching bad things happen to others or absorbing the anxiety of those around us can also embed fear in our subconscious.

Fear itself isn't inherently bad. It's a basic emotion meant to protect us by signaling danger. It's healthy to feel some anxiety—it keeps us alert and cautious. However, when fear becomes irrational and starts to disrupt daily life, it's time to address it.

"Every thought you think affects you both physically and emotionally." This truth highlights how avoidance and negative thought patterns can intensify fear, while positive experiences and gradual exposure can help reduce it.

The Power of Your Thoughts

"Every thought you think affects you both physically and emotionally." This truth underscores how our mental patterns can amplify fear or calm it. Avoidance tends to magnify fear, while positive, reassuring experiences can reduce it.

Remember: "Every thought you think affects you both physically and emotionally."

Coping with various fears

1. Physical Fears
These include fears of heights, animals, or medical procedures.
- **How to Cope:** Gradual exposure, paired with relaxation techniques, can help desensitize physical fears. For example, if you fear needles, start by imagining the scenario calmly, then progress to watching videos or holding a syringe in a non-threatening setting. Deep breathing and visualization can help keep your body relaxed during these steps.

2. Emotional Fears
These include fears of vulnerability, rejection, or expressing emotions.
- **How to Cope:** Practice emotional resilience by journaling, talking with trusted friends, or working with a therapist. Reframe your thoughts by focusing on self-compassion and understanding that vulnerability is a strength, not a weakness.

3. Mental Fears
These include fears of failure, success, or losing control.
- **How to Cope:** Replace limiting beliefs with empowering affirmations. Break large challenges into smaller, manageable steps to reduce overwhelm. Mindfulness meditation can help quiet mental chatter and bring focus to the present moment.

4. Relationship Fears

These include fears of abandonment, intimacy, or conflict.

- **How to Cope:** Open communication is key. Express your fears to your partner or a trusted individual. Learn to set healthy boundaries and practice active listening. Therapy can also help unpack past experiences that contribute to these fears and create a healthier outlook on relationships.

Unlearning fears

Releasing fear begins with acknowledging it without judgment. Recognize it as a signal, not a permanent state. Allow yourself to feel it, but don't let it define you. Focus on your breath, ground yourself in the present, and replace fearful thoughts with empowering ones.

Phobias, while overwhelming, are among the easiest psychological challenges to treat. Even severe fears can often be resolved in a few focused sessions using techniques like desensitization and relaxation.

You are not alone!

Whether your fear is physical, emotional, mental, or relational, remember this: you are not weak, broken, or alone. Fear is part of being human, but it doesn't have to control you. With the right tools and support, you can release fear, regain your confidence, and reclaim your freedom.

Practical Steps to Overcoming Phobias

If you fall off a horse, you've probably heard the advice to get back on right away. This principle also applies to phobias. Gradual exposure, paired with relaxation techniques, can help desensitize your fear over time.

For example:
1. Begin by practicing small steps toward the object or situation that frightens you.
2. Stay relaxed as you face your fear, bit by bit until it loses its hold.

Relaxation: a tool for freedom

Learning to relax is a vital part of overcoming fear and phobias. Techniques like deep breathing, progressive muscle relaxation, and mindfulness can help calm your body and mind. As you stay relaxed and gradually expose yourself to the feared object or situation, your fear will naturally diminish.

Let's take that step together. You've got this.

What you think – You create.
What you feel – You attract.
What you imagine – You become.
"You Matter" ~ Liza

SELF ACTUALIZATION

Discover Your Reoccurring Patterns

Self-actualization is the journey of becoming who you were always meant to be, a path that reveals itself through honest self-reflection and a commitment to growth. Yet, to fully realize this, it's essential to understand the patterns you unconsciously repeat in your life—those recurring thoughts and behaviors that, often unknowingly, shape where you are today. Recognizing these patterns is the first step toward breaking free from anything that no longer serves you and moving toward a life aligned with your deepest desires and strengths.

To do this exercise, start by finding a quiet place, one where you can truly reflect. Grab a pen and paper and permit yourself to be entirely truthful. Self-awareness requires us to leave past judgments behind, so we can step forward with a clear mind and an open heart. Take a moment to set an intention: you are here to explore your thoughts and feelings without judgment, to understand what has brought you to this point, and to envision what might lead you toward a life of fulfillment and purpose.

The journey begins now, with honesty, reflection, and a willingness to let go. Here are a few questions to guide you as you uncover the patterns that have shaped your life and prepare to set a new course.

Key questions to ask yourself:
- ❖ What thoughts of mine have contributed to where my life is today?
- ❖ What new ways can I think of to shift my life to what I desire it to be?
- ❖ How will reaching my goals change my life?
- ❖ What are my strengths, and how can I use them to serve myself best?

I am now willing to release the patterns within me that created this condition. Use verbal affirmations to make strong positive statements that what you want already exists. Compose your affirmations according to your own needs. Use the first person, present tense, state your affirmations positively, and watch the results as you grow and prosper.

Affirmations:

- I release fear and welcome courage into my heart.
- With every breath, I let go of what holds me back and embrace my inner strength.
- I trust in my ability to overcome any challenge.
- Fear is a passing emotion; my courage is constant and powerful.
- I am safe, grounded, and capable in every situation.
- I choose thoughts that uplift and empower me.
- I grow more confident and fearless.
- I am in control of my mind, body, and emotions.
- My past does not define me; I create a fearless and fulfilling future.
- I can safely express my thoughts and feelings.
- I am brave, resilient, and unstoppable.
- I am worthy of giving and receiving love.
- I am loving and lovable.
- I do my best and my best is good enough.
- I trust myself and others in loving relationships.
- I create abundance by doing what I love.
- I deserve prosperity and success.
- I easily ask for what I need—and expect to get it.
- I will learn to better myself.
- I MATTER

Repeat these affirmations daily to reprogram your mind, calm your fears, and cultivate self-empowerment.

*"The breath is the cord that ties the soul to the body.
Become aware of it, and you reclaim your power."*
~ Dr. Wayne Dyer

Mind/Body Visualization

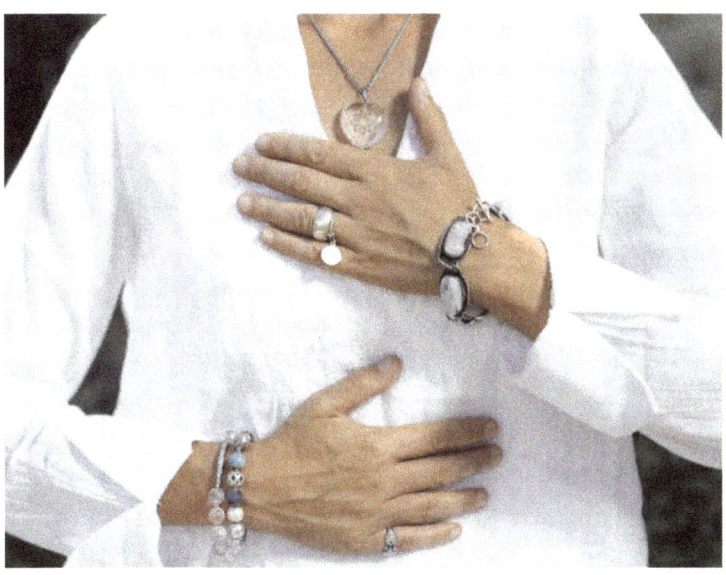

Take a deep breath and close your eyes. Now imagine being inside your mind. Notice what that space looks or feels like. What's your sense of this space? Imagine a switch in this space. It can be any size or shape. This switch allows your muscles to let go so that you can relax even more deeply than before.

Whenever you turn off this switch, your muscles relax instantly. Find your switch now, and when you are ready, turn it off. Remember that you're in complete control and can turn it back on whenever you want... Notice how much more relaxed you are when the switch is off.

There is another switch in this room. This switch slows down and quiets your thoughts. Locate this switch now and, when you are ready, turn it off. Take a few minutes to enjoy this deep relaxation. Now, when you are ready, turn the switch back on.

Image Rehearsal

This allows you to practice a new behavior in a safe setting. If you want to feel calmer and more in control, then see yourself with that behavior.

If visualization doesn't come naturally, you're not alone! Many people find it challenging to see clear images in their mind's eye, but there are gentle ways to begin building this skill. Start by tapping into your other senses—imagine what something *feels* like, what it would sound like, or even the subtle smells in the scene. Instead of straining to "see" a vivid picture, focus on the emotions you'd feel if your vision were real.

For instance, if you're visualizing yourself on a peaceful beach, feel the warmth of the sun on your skin, the relaxation in your body, and hear the waves, even if you can't quite "see" them.

Visualization is all about capturing the essence of the experience, not just the image. Practice these little moments daily with kindness and patience toward yourself. Take a deep breath and close your eyes. Form a clear picture of the new scene. Notice your surroundings and fill in as many details as you can. Notice what you are wearing. Feel all the emotions. Fully experience this new behavior. Notice how good it feels to act and react the way you want. You are in complete control of your responses.

Let go of the need for perfect clarity and simply invite whatever details to come naturally. With time, you'll find that your ability to imagine deepens, allowing you to connect with your vision in a meaningful way.

Write down how you would like to act at work, at school, with family or friends. What is the change you'd like to make and feel about yourself? Use as much detail as you can. If you want to feel calmer, think about what circumstances and which persons you need to feel calmer.

Finish up your scene now and remember where you are in the room. Take a deep breath and open your eyes.

> *"It's not about the goal. It's about growing to become the person that can accomplish that goal."* ~ Tony Robbins

BEING HAPPY IS A STATE OF MIND

We read and hear about this all the time, about how we have to "control" our emotions, and how some emotions are "negative." Emotions are simply feelings, and these feelings are information about what's happening within. Angry, happy, sad, scared, and bored are messages from the inner voice suggesting courses of action, and trying to censor or determine what information comes along inevitably leads to confusion, guilt, disease, self-destruction or hatred, and possibly substance abuse. Overeating is the number one numbing means for uncomfortable emotions, followed by overwork, alcohol, and tobacco.

While we cannot control our emotions nor should we want to, we can influence them with the only thing in life that we do have total control over – our thoughts. We can only be responsible for our actions and reactions, which include our thinking.

Instead of chasing "happiness" let us experience the balance of human life while staying connected to and respectful of our inner voice.

For instance, if we choose to obsess about the imaginary future, trying to cover every possible turn of events unknown to us, then fear and worry will follow that stagnated thinking and suffocate us. On the other hand, if we take a calm or mindful approach to plan and focus our thoughts on the wonders of the moment – our emotions will consequently relate to the flow of the moment. To do this, we must build inner confidence to handle whatever new adventure confronts us.

Hypnotherapy can help you regain your confidence and be more connected to your true core self – creating joy within.

"We all live with the objective of being happy, or lives are all different and yet the same." ~ Anne Frank

Evolve

GUIDED RELAXATION

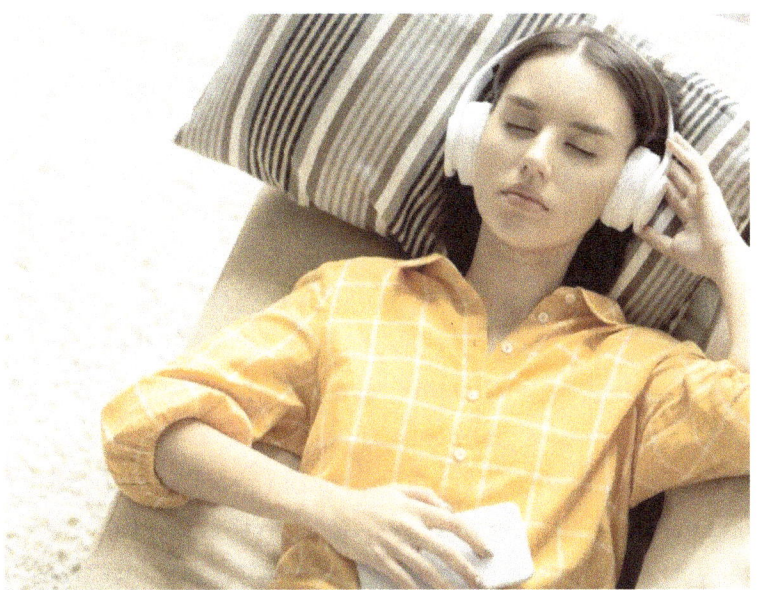

Start by making yourself comfortable in any way that you would like. You may sit up or lie down. Make sure that your head, neck, and body are fully supported.

Take a full and deep breath. Inhale through your nostrils and exhale through your mouth. Imagine that each time you inhale, you bring in oxygen and vitality into your body, and as you exhale, you allow all anxiety and stress to come out of your body as you blow them away. Close your eyes and keep them closed.

Imagine in your mind looking down at your feet. Allow all the muscles and the nerves around each toe to relax. Now relax your feet. Allow all the muscles and the nerves in your feet to become very relaxed. So relaxed that you may find that you don't even want to move them. So relaxed that you don't even care about moving them. With each breath that you take, you become more relaxed.

So relaxed that you may drift deeper and deeper into this deep relaxation. Now allow the same relaxed and heavy sensation that started at your toes and flowed to your feet, now flowing into your entire leg. Your legs may become so heavy that they may feel like heavy lead weights. So heavy that you may find that you cannot move them very readily. As you allow this relaxation to come up, you realize your entire lower portion is relaxing even more. Now with every breath that you take, the deeper you relax. You relax and as you do this deep focusing of awareness, the heavy and relaxed feeling flows upwards to your entire upper body - up to your abdominal muscles, your chest muscles relax.

That's right. The more you relax, your awareness deepens. Now the same relaxed feeling goes through your chest down into your left arm down to your fingertips. And your whole left arm feels very relaxed, so relaxed that you find that you don't care to move your arm. So relaxed that the relaxation just flows into your right hand and down to your fingertips. By now, you may feel a tingling or pulsating sensation at the tip of your fingers. With each breath that you take, the deeper you relax.

All the heavy sensations indicate that you are becoming very relaxed. You will feel utterly relaxed throughout your body. Now let the same relaxation in your right arm, hand, and fingers flow down your left hand and into your left fingers. Both arms are now completely relaxed, you let the same relaxation flow into the rest of your body. Your shoulders, your neck, your face, and your scalp, then down your back.

Every muscle and nerve is completely and comfortably relaxed. And as this wonderful feeling of relaxation spreads throughout your entire body, check to make sure each muscle is totally and completely relaxed. Now with a growing sense of comfort, satisfaction, and enjoyment, you know how easy it is to learn about going into a deep, relaxed state.

When thinking positive and loving thoughts, your energy and focus will be drawn to the positive, and loving, and you will focus more on the positives, which further enables you to stay relaxed. By staying in a relaxed and tension-free state as much as possible, your body will promote further health and overall well-being.

> *"For those who believe, No proof is necessary.*
> *For those who don't believe, No proof is possible."*
> ~ Stuart Chase

CONNECTING WITH YOUR HIGHER SELF THROUGH SPIRITUAL MEDITATION

Spiritual meditation is a powerful tool to connect with your higher self and tap into the wisdom and guidance within you. It is a journey of self-discovery, transformation, and deeper spiritual awareness that leads to clarity, peace, and alignment with your true self.

When you connect with your higher self, you gain access to intuitive wisdom and a greater understanding of your life's purpose. This connection fosters inner peace, empowerment, and a sense of balance, allowing you to live authentically and intentionally.

Techniques for Spiritual Meditation

1. **Breathwork and Visualization**
   Find a quiet space, close your eyes, and take slow, deep breaths. As you inhale, visualize pure, positive energy entering your body. As you exhale, release tension and negativity. Imagine this energy nourishing every cell, bringing calm and relaxation.
2. **Mantras and Affirmations**
   Repeat a meaningful mantra or affirmation that resonates with your spiritual intention, such as "I am connected to my higher self" or "I am open to divine guidance." Allow the positive vibrations to align you with your inner wisdom.
3. **Mindfulness and Presence**
   Practice mindfulness by bringing your awareness to the

present moment. Observe your thoughts and emotions without judgment. Focus on your breath or the sensations in your body to quiet the mind and create space for spiritual connection.
4. **Gratitude and Intention Setting**
Begin your meditation by expressing gratitude and setting a clear intention. This could be to deepen your connection with your higher self, find clarity, or invite spiritual guidance. Gratitude creates a receptive mindset for spiritual growth.

Practical Steps for Spiritual Meditation

1. **Find a Quiet Space:** Choose a calm, distraction-free environment.
2. **Set Your Intention:** Reflect on what you want to achieve or connect with during your meditation.
3. **Breathe Deeply:** Focus on your breath to relax and center yourself.
4. **Visualize Connection:** Imagine a loving light above your head, symbolizing your higher self, and let it envelop you with wisdom and peace.
5. **Repeat Affirmations:** Use affirmations or mantras to strengthen your focus and intention.

6. **Embrace Stillness:** Allow yourself to simply be present, releasing distractions and finding clarity in silence.
7. **Express Gratitude:** End your meditation with gratitude for the insights and connections you've cultivated.

Integrating Spiritual Meditation into Daily Life

- **Morning Intentions:** Start your day with a mindful intention to align with your higher self.
- **Gratitude Practice:** Reflect on your blessings daily to cultivate positivity and awareness.
- **Mindful Moments:** Pause throughout the day to breathe, center yourself, and connect with your inner guidance.
- **Evening Reflection:** Dedicate time each night to review your day, express gratitude, and set intentions for tomorrow.

Spiritual meditation is a deeply personal journey. Adapt these practices to your unique needs and preferences. As you connect with your higher self, you'll discover clarity, peace, and the ability to live more authentically.

UNLOAD STRESS OVERLOAD

Unloading head junk may be the most important and lasting way to lower your daily stress load.

Head junk includes all the negative and constantly draining thoughts, emotions, and beliefs you carry around in your head regularly. All the past doubts, harsh criticisms, and "could have"/"should haves". It is this undercurrent of troubling self-talk that keeps your worry, upset, discouragement, frustration, and self-directed anger perpetually bubbling just under the surface.

If you permit self-defeating, negative thoughts and feelings to build up, consciously or unconsciously, your mental distress storage will fill to the brim. Then, when other annoyances, fears, or threats arise, your storage overflows. It is difficult to cope with much when you feel under the gun, stressed out, and overwhelmed. If your storage is always at this point, then you may struggle with feeling depressed, anxious, and angry, or on the constant edge in anticipation of another setback. This is when the mind and body can shut down, only to protect you. The circuit breaker trips.

To take charge of your emotional state, let the negative feelings get reduced or eliminated, allowing everyday stressors to become easier to handle. By reducing emotional and sensory overload, more energy and mental reserves are available to dream and go for what you want in life. You become more resilient and better able to cope with challenging times.

Your inner mind loves to learn and integrate new ideas, finding solutions to erase and transform old patterns into new ones. Creating healthier and empowering habits and rituals brings forth desires you intend to make both internally and externally.

The Elevator Metaphor:

Perhaps the following metaphor provides another perspective. Let's imagine you are standing in an elevator and the buttons on the panel are called stress buttons, with you having total control over the buttons.

Now, what if you decide one or more of the buttons leading to certain floors are out of order, and no matter who or what were to push these buttons, it'll go nowhere, no matter how hard it's pushed? The light does not come on; thus the elevator does not go anywhere.

Simply, it makes no difference to you. Just as if you are immune to the stressors until you, and only you, turn them back on. You take control of not only this situation, but all situations until you are ready to react or respond accordingly, and in a healthier way. Being the operator of your elevator!

It's a wonderful feeling to confront face-to-face with someone or perceive something that once controlled you, triggering mental or physical distress, and can now face it calmly with little or no reaction or effort.

You have the power to progress, heal, and evolve! With practice, it becomes easier to control which "floors" your elevator travels to. People and circumstances that induced stress will become things of the past—distant memories.

Power of Words

Changing low-energy words to high-frequency, empowering ones can significantly uplift your mindset and energy.

Shifting how you speak not only changes your perspective but also rewires your subconscious to respond with positivity and strength. Here's a list of common low-energy words and their higher-frequency replacements:

Low-Energy to High-Frequency Word Swaps

1. **Worry → Concern**
   Instead of "I worry about my health," say, "I have a concern about my health, and I'm addressing it."
2. **Problem → Challenge**
   o "This challenge gives me allows me" instead of "This problem is overwhelming."
3. **Stress → Effort**
   o Replace "This is stressing me out" with "This requires effort, and I can handle it."
4. **Failure → Lesson**

- "I learned a valuable lesson," instead of "I feel like a failure."
5. **Overwhelmed → Fully Engaged**
    - "I'm fully engaged in this task," instead of "I'm overwhelmed with work."
6. **Busy → Productive**
    - "I've been productive today," rather than "I'm so busy today."
7. **Hard → Unfamiliar**
    - "This task feels unfamiliar," instead of "This is so hard."
8. **Stuck → Exploring**
    - "I'm exploring new possibilities," instead of "I'm stuck in this situation."
9. **Loss → Letting Go**
    - : "I'm letting go of what no longer serves me," instead of "I'm experiencing a loss."
10. **Alone → Independent**
    - "I value my independence," instead of "I feel so alone."

"Your thoughts are powerful because they become the words you speak, and the words you speak create the world you live in. Change your self-talk, and you change your life." ~ Dr. Joe Dispenza

RELAXATION TECHNIQUES

Healing with Water

This exercise is ideally done under the shower, where water acts as the clearing waterfall. Let the flowing water clear away the worries and anxieties of the day. Let all thoughts or memories that may have been causing you discomfort wash away. Visualize it dropping, washing, and falling away from you in glistening droplets, and watch it go down the drain.

Water will clear negative energies and restore balance to your body, which has been affected by them. Washing is a process of cleansing, symbolic of an inner clearing, and preparing you for a fresh start.

Let the water wash away the pain and burdens weighing on your back, and when you turn and face the faucet, let it wash away your tears. For injured muscles or arthritis turn the knob to cold for two minutes – it helps tired muscles recover and awaken the body.

Boost Your Immune System

Recognizing your well-being depends on how you care for yourself.

1. Acknowledge your weaknesses and turn them into positive mental expectations.
2. Understand that your feelings, your thoughts, and the images you hold in your conscious and subconscious mind ultimately act and determine the course that you take in life.
3. Don't solve problems by looking to blame anyone else. It's a waste of time. *Find solutions* to problems within yourself.
4. Allow yourself to become the authority figure in your life.
5. Take responsibility for yourself, your choices, your actions, and your outcomes.
6. Accept yourself deeply and completely as you are.

LAUGHTER IS GOOD MEDICINE

Laughter is so important. I am not talking about a smile here and there, but pure joy and laughter. When was the last time you laughed so hard that tears started flowing down your face? Remember that time? I bet you can't even remember what it was for – but you sure do remember the scene. Was it that long ago? I want you to know that you have the same joy within you right now.

Let's bring that joy back to your everyday life and being!

They say laughter is the best remedy for all illnesses...Dr. Norman Cousins fended off a life-threatening disease using his regimen of nutritional and emotional support as opposed to traditional methods of treatment. Cousins are often described as "the man who laughed his way to health!" Did you know that for every minute of laughter, you produce somewhere around $10,000 worth of healthy body chemistry?!

Laughter operates on at least three different levels. They are the biophysical, the biochemical, and the bioenergetics levels. Laughter moves lymph and oxygenates your organs at the biophysical level. It moves lymph fluid around your body simply by the convulsions you experience during the process of laughing, so it boosts immune system function and helps clear out old, dead waste products from organs and tissues.

Laughter increases the oxygenation of your body at both the cellular and organ levels. By laughing, in gulps, you take in vast amounts of oxygen. It's also interesting to note that cancer cells are destroyed in the presence of oxygen. Many parasites and bacteria don't survive well in the presence of oxygen, and to the extent that you can circulate extra oxygen throughout your body, you can help prevent, or in some cases treat these diseases.

Laughing also boosts circulation. The harder you laugh, the greater this effect. If you can find a way to put yourself into a state of rolling, outrageous laughter, you're going to get a fantastic physical workout from it! Have you ever laughed so hard that your stomach hurts and your facial muscles are exhausted? That's some serious exercise, and it's the kind of exercise in which we should all engage regularly.

TALK THE TALK

You can use self-hypnosis as well as affirmations to increase your desire for healthy foods that burn off fat and give you lots of energy while improving your health. You can use the following affirmations to realize your healthy living goals:

- I enjoy being physically active.
- I feel strong and healthy.
- I enjoy at least 20 minutes of exercise a day.
- I easily drink at least six glasses of water a day.
- I feel renewed and reenergized with each step I take.
- I see the weight disappearing as I exercise.
- I have heightened senses as I exercise my body.
- I feel stress disappear when I focus on my body.

Healthy Exercise for Healthy Living

Take a walk with your dog, play some ball or go swimming with your kids, dance in your living room for twenty minutes, take a walk around the block during your lunch break, or hike your favorite mountain trail. Let go of your limiting beliefs. Go beyond what was. Move forward by discovering your quest and living in the world you dreamt of - Say YES to you.

Get Motivated

Getting off the couch and into the gym is half the battle - 20 to 30 minutes per day, three to six times a week, is recommended.

Uplift Your Habits

Changing routine may not be as easy, yet necessary. What worked in the past may not be serving you today - everything from eating to working, from parenting to making love. Uplifting your mood and shifting your thoughts can lead you to be in the best shape while living a purposeful, fulfilled life.

TIPS TO LIVING HEALTHIER AND HAPPIER

1. Create a ritual: Write down your to-do list and check off three essentials to do each day.
2. Make a list of things that you love to do and post the list on your bathroom mirror.
3. Consciously surround yourself with supportive and positive people you like who inspire you and you enjoy being around.
4. Praise and reward yourself and your loved ones.
5. Speak in 'the now' – as if it is happening. "I am thinner."
6. Take a break and relax.
7. Let go of self-criticism and petty stuff.
8. Use empowering words such as Good, Exciting, Joy, Success, and I love You.

9. Hug more – let someone you care about know they mean so much to you.

Setting meaningful goals is a powerful step toward personal growth and success, but achieving them often requires more than just determination—it's about surrounding yourself with the right people. When you align with those who lift you, inspire you, and genuinely support your journey, you create an environment where you can thrive. These are the people who celebrate your wins, encourage you through challenges, and remind you of your worth when self-doubt creeps in.

By choosing to be with individuals who radiate positivity and share your values, you build a network of empowerment that propels you toward your dreams with confidence and resilience.

You can also create a list of all the things you intend to do, feel, create, and achieve. Change your words and it'll shift your thoughts. And when you shift your thoughts, you can change your life.

You Matter!

FOODS TO KEEP YOU HEALTHY, FRUITY, NUTTY

Lemon: Drinking a glass of (warm) water with freshly squeezed lemon in the morning is a great way to hydrate and wake up your entire digestive system.

Blueberries: Their antioxidant powers make them a refreshing fruit for your whole body, and their muscle-building abilities are just what you'll need for those summer workouts.

Peanuts: These nutty treats boost your energy and lower your cholesterol. They're great for your skin and hair, and a polyphenolic antioxidant makes peanuts an awesome cancer preventive.

Watermelon: It's not summer until that first bite into a juicy slice of watermelon. Packed with antioxidants like vitamin C, beta carotene, and lycopene, it's a perfect thirst quencher on a hot summer day.

Cherries: Tart and sweet cherries. They're an excellent source of anthocyanins and fiber. Their vitamin C and flavonoids help cherries fight cancer-causing agents. They've also been shown to lower inflammation in the body thanks to their phytochemicals.

Almonds: These nuts are not only scrumptious but energy-producing. Their vitamin E helps the brain function and focus. They also lower the risk of heart disease, high blood pressure, and weight gain.

Avocados: This delicious sunshine fruit is full of fats and oils that your body needs. The oleic acid in avocados helps your digestive system work better to absorb carotenoids, a powerful antioxidant also found in carrots and spinach. Adding an avocado to a salad with spinach and carrots can increase your carotenoid absorption by 200%-400%.

Eggs: Eggs offer several benefits for both the mind and body, including being a rich source of protein and choline. Choline is crucial for brain development and function, supporting learning, memory, and neurotransmitter synthesis. Eggs also provide important vitamins and minerals like Vitamin D, B vitamins, and folate, which are linked to brain health, heart health, and overall well-being

You are what you eat, and you control who you are.
Thus you can control what you eat

.

GRATITUDE – Thankful Mediation

Grateful or Gratitude Mediation. This form of meditation allows your body to settle into a state of profound rest and your mind to achieve a state of inner peace and joy.

Quiet time slows our minds, calms our spirits, and centers our souls. It removes our mind from clutter and outside hassles that surround us and centers us on something greater and more fulfilling. It provides an opportunity to identify our desires, articulate our values, and align our pursuits accordingly. In quiet and solitude, our mind gravitates towards the more important things—the most valuable. We naturally focus on our souls, our families, our friends, our health, our significance, and our greatest ambitions.

You can do this by carving out some time for yourself. Sit back (back supported with a pillow), uncross your legs and fingers, and gently close your eyes - (we see more with our eyes closed). Become aware of your breath, sounds, smells... feel a sense of calmness within. You are safe.

Now allow your mind to wander and imagine as if you are watching a movie, "This is your life". Go back in time. Imagine seeing the timeline of all your actions, reactions, feelings, thoughts, and experiences. Become more aware and grateful for living through them. Simply acknowledge what was and be present for what is today. Now you can choose to make changes for the better. Project what you desire in your life – how you want to feel. Immerse yourself in how this new image will make you feel better, stronger, healthier, happier, successful, etc.

Stay with the feeling – Breathe through it – Own it
If you do this several minutes a week, you will find that your celebration of You is richer and fuller than you have imagined it could be. You might just discover that your overall happiness with life improves. Imagine your goal as if you've reached it. How does it look? How does it feel? Now, hold that feeling for a couple of seconds or minutes. Feels great, right? It is inspiring knowing that you can see within your mind the goal reached.

LIZA'S '33 DAY' HABIT FORMING THEORY:

You may have heard the phrase "It takes 21 days to form a habit." Liza's philosophy is that it takes '33 consecutive days of repeating the same thing over and over – either good or bad- to change and form a new habit. Are you wondering why 33 instead of 21 days? We are creatures of habit and function in a society where everything is measured by "time."

This means - we know and understand seconds, minutes, hours, days, weeks, and months. Most days in a month are 31. If we continue a new routine for over 33 consecutive days, then we have done it for over an entire month and are already into the next month. Most think and feel, "If I can do it for over a month, I wonder if I can do this again for the next 33 days," thus placing the new programming into action for the third month.

It is quite simple; instead of coming short in the month (21 days), you have now accomplished something you did not believe imaginable. While your entire thought process was to do something for 33 days continually, the pressure and the discomfort of "possible failure" is lifted ...and by the second month, the new habit is formed! Bingo! You've succeeded and conquered the old habit. Saying to yourself: "I did it" - "it worked"! Success feeds success! And what is "it"? IT is YOU.

You have and have had the Power Within all along. For some unknown reason, if this method does not work, we then use hypnosis to find out what other underlying blocks have been lingering within our subconscious mind in need of change. We work to help you feel better, drop negative habits, and begin your new lifestyle of wellness in mind and body. If the intent and the desire are present, then Change is easily achieved!

For best results, **we highly recommend** you purchase the audio recordings specifically narrated for *Heal-thy Mind-Body.*" By listening to Liza Boubari's *Relax and Unwind* recording, you can let it all go and become a healthier you! Use this recording at the end of every day for 33 consecutive days to promote lasting results.

Go to https://healwithin.com/shop to find "Relax and Unwind" along with other helpful audio recordings.

YOUR COLORS

Did you know colors evoke certain emotions?
Have you noticed that when you feel gloomy, if you wear something brighter, you'll feel a bit better and lighten up your mood?

"He saw red."
"I'm feeling blue."
"She was green with envy."

How often have you heard these expressions? They're fairly common. And they're a good illustration of how color relates to our emotions.

Color evokes a physical effect on the human body. It can influence the pituitary gland, which helps regulate hormone production. Hormones can affect our moods, so it makes sense that color would, too. But it can also be used to change our moods and self-perceptions. How can you use colors to change your mood? Well, clothing is the most obvious choice. What you wear not only helps you feel a certain way but also can give a strong impression of your confidence to others, especially people you've never met.

Below is a breakdown of how each primary color makes you feel.

- **Red:** – Root – grounding. Associated with Love, Heat, evokes Anger, Intensity, and Excitement. Red is used to increase circulation and stimulate the body and mind.
- **Orange:** – Sexuality – Energetic, Warm color, evokes Enthusiasm and Excitement. Orange is used to draw attention, as in traffic signs.
- **Yellow:** – Solar- Digestion. Cheery, Warm, Core, Nature, but evokes Frustration and Anger. Yellow increases metabolism. Highly visible, attention-grabber.
- **Green:** – Heart – Emotions. Nature, Health, Healing, Good Luck, Tranquility, and Jealousy have been known to increase the ability to read, used in decorating to relieve stress and calm, the color of fertility.
- **Blue:** Throat – Calm, Relaxed, Soothing; evokes Serenity, Sadness – Men Preferred, Research-proven blue rooms make people more productive; least appetizing. Blue can ease the suffering of illness and pain and also lower the pulse and body temperature.
- **Violet/Purple:** – Third-eye. Symbol of Wealth and Royalty, Spirituality, and Wisdom. Sometimes evokes: exotic, mysterious.

- **White:** – Crown – Innocence, Spacious, Purity, Sterile, Focus, isolation
- **Black** may make some people think of depression, but it doesn't have to. It's a very dramatic color; many artists wear nothing but black. It can denote mystery, something hidden – or maybe an introvert who's been around crowds too long could use it to "hide" from people. In this sense, it can be a very classy or protective color.
- **Gray** is a common color for business suits, and in those instances, it can indicate independence, self-control, and self-confidence. But some color specialists think it's also about ambiguity and indecision; after all, it isn't black, and it isn't white, either.

You don't have to change everything about your appearance to benefit from color confidence. Sometimes an accessory, like a tie or scarf, in a particular color will have the desired effect, without being too noticeable to others. Many of my friends know I enjoy wearing scarves and Pashmina and have a vast collection of different designs and colors. I enjoy the feeling of comfort and coziness, as it enhances the look of my wardrobe.

You may also want to make changes to your surroundings. This doesn't mean, though, that you have to replace all your wardrobe or furniture (unless you want to, of course!). Small changes like fresh flowers, decorations, pillows, or other throws placed on the furniture may just do the trick!

Your Vision is Our Mission - 'You Matter'

You Matter

- Are you now ready to <u>Acknowledge</u> the issues, problems, or blocks that you want to change?
- Are you now ready to <u>Accept</u> your present situation due to your past behaviors or habits you learned, mimicked, and acquired, either knowingly or unknowingly?
- Are you now ready to take <u>Action</u>, step up, and take responsibility for resolving or overcoming said issues, problems, or blocks that are no longer necessary or beneficial to you?
- Are you now ready to Be the Change and Live an Extraordinary Life-Victoriously? If so, say **YES**! **Yes, 'I Matter'**.

We strive to stand by you in your journey toward self-renewal and inner healing. Acknowledge, discover, heal, and transform yourself. You deserve to blossom and bloom from the inside out. Our Philosophy: Nurture – We provide solutions to help you live a better and well-balanced life.

Our environment is designed to nurture you from the minute you enter our healing center. Educate – Knowledge is power. It is our responsibility to pass on our understanding and years of experience in healing, so that you may grasp our healing process on a much deeper level.

As you are empowered, your impact on others will continually transform your life! Believe what your heart and gut tell you, not what others say. Trust your gut, but make decisions with your mind.

Your journey to a healthier mind and body starts here. Together, we'll uncover what's holding you back, embrace your present reality, and create the life you truly desire. With my guidance and the transformative tools in *Heal-Thy Mind-Body*, you'll gain the clarity, insight, and strength to confidently move forward.

Contact me today for a personalized consultation.

BONUS: A GENTLE SELF-HYPNOSIS PRACTICE FOR DEEPER HEALING

Instructions for Self-Hypnosis Practice

All hypnosis is self-hypnosis.

You may read and record this script slowly in your own voice and listen before sleep.

When your own voice speaks with calm and intention, it becomes ten times more nurturing and impactful.

Your subconscious receives it as truth — especially during quiet moments of rest.

After you record it:

Find a quiet, comfortable space where you will not be disturbed.

Sit or recline in a way that feels fully supported.

When ready, gently close your eyes and begin listening to your recording.

Self-Hypnosis: Restore Inner Harmony

Now that I am still...

I return to the quiet wisdom within.

I breathe gently and allow my body to settle.

With each breath, I soften my thoughts.

With each exhale, I release the tension that has lingered too long.

I acknowledge the stress I've held—physical, emotional, or unspoken.

And I now give myself permission to let go of what is no longer mine to carry.

I am ready to accept and appreciate myself—just as I am.

Even when I did not understand it, I know my body has tried to protect me.

And now, I lovingly guide it toward healing.

I allow peace to move through me.

I release resistance.

I release fear.

I release the pressure to be anything other than myself.

I restore calm in my mind.

I restore flow in my body.

I restore trust

ABOUT LIZA

Why the Boubari 3E Method Works

Liza Boubari is a Certified Clinical Hypnotherapist and creator of the Boubari 3E Method. With over two decades of experience, she's helped countless individuals heal and transform their lives, specializing in smoking cessation and stress reduction.

"Life changed for me when I learned to connect my mind and body to heal from within." Liza's journey of overcoming health challenges fuels her mission to guide others in achieving lasting transformation.

With Heal-Thy Mind-Body, Liza combines guided imagery, empowering affirmations, and intentional insights to guide readers in reclaiming their health, peace, and inner balance. Her professional expertise and compassionate approach have empowered countless individuals to heal emotional wounds, reduce stress, and live healthier, more fulfilling lives.

As the host of RealTalk870 on AM870 Talk Radio, Liza empowers listeners each Sunday at 10 PM to explore mental wellness, emotional stability, and the mind-body connection through inspiring conversations and expert interviews.

"Our eyes are not only to see – but to project what we witness." – Liza

The work you have done is a testament to your courage and commitment. Trust that you are exactly where you need to be, guided by a higher energy that has always been within you. Take the first step toward healing within—you're worth it.

Book your session today at HealWithin. I encourage you to get the *Relax and Unwind* self-hypnosis audio to reinforce your journey. Visit **HealWithin.com** for resources, tools, and more inspirational success stories.

Our Mission:

To empower individuals to heal within by uncovering and transforming layers of hurt and pain buried deep in the unconscious mind.
Evoke - Embrace - Evolve – You Matter

If you or someone you know is ready to begin the journey of healing mind and body, reach out for a free, no-obligation consultation. Take the first step toward creating a healthier, happier you. Let's start your journey of healing today.

Contact Us:
📞 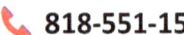 818-551-1501
🌐 www.lizabobuari.com
🌐 www.healwithin.com

www.ingramcontent.com/pod-product-compliance
Lightning Source LLC
LaVergne TN
LVHW021948060526
838200LV00043B/1961